JOURNAL

Compiled by Patti M. Hummel

B&H
PUBLISHING GROUP
Nashville, Tennessee

For the word of God is living and effective and sharper than any double-edged sword, . . . able to judge the thoughts and intentions of the heart.—Hebrews 4:12

God's Word is a gift with power to expose our imperfections, to show us how to be more holy, teach us about our Savior, and protect us from our enemy.—Josiah McGee, 15; Kansas City, MO; Summit Woods Baptist Church

_____

_____

_____

_____

_____

_____

_____

_____

_____

_____

_____

_____

_____

_____

_____

_____

_____

_____

_____

_____

*During the hard times in my life I learned not to base what I
thought about God on my feelings but on the truth of His Word. I
had to cling to the truth that He is exactly who He says He is, no
matter what, always, and forever!*—McKenzie Sutton, 17; Waverly Hall,
GA; Cornerstone Baptist Church

Trust in the LORD with all your heart, and do not rely on your own understanding; in all your ways know him, and he will make your paths straight.—Proverbs 3:5–6

[If you] trust in God, He will lead you in the right path. God's ways are the best ways, and He won't lead you to where you don't need to be.—Nolan Martin, 16; Marshville, NC; Mount Moriah Baptist Church

A lot of teenagers struggle with trust problems. . . . God has everything in the palm of His hand, so why not trust Him?

—Megan Medford, 14; Bryant, AR; The Church at Rock Creek

We all run into problems and questions at some time in our lives, but we need to remember Matthew 7:7 and Proverbs 3:5 so that we can ask for the answer, seek it out, and trust that God will do what is right in our life.—Clayton Alexander Teal, 17; Pageland, SC; Smyrna Baptist Church

He has told each of you . . . what it is the LORD requires of you: to act justly, to love faithfulness, and to walk humbly with your God.—Micah 6:8

Keep your thoughts focused on God and His Word, asking Him to help you. The results and growth in Him will amaze you. . . . Focus on Jesus and His promises because He can be trusted to help.

—Robby D. Land, 18; Gatlinburg, TN; First Baptist Church

I will instruct you and show you the way to go; with my eye on you, I will give counsel.—Psalm 32:8

_____

_____

_____

_____

_____

_____

_____

_____

_____

_____

_____

_____

_____

_____

_____

_____

_____

_____

_____

_____

_____

_____

_____

_____

_____

_____

_____

_____

_____

_____

_____

_____

_____

_____

_____

_____

_____

_____

_____

_____

_____

_____

_____

_____

_____

_____

The Bible is like a guide for life and helps everyone to take on hardships with better wisdom and agility.—Abby Fortner, 15; Gatlinburg, TN; First Baptist Church

When arrogance comes, disgrace follows, but with humility comes wisdom.—Proverbs 11:2

An acorn must first bury itself beneath the earth with all of its commotion and destruction in order to be nurtured into a great tree that will give comfort, peace, and nourishment to the world around it.—Brady Fowlkes, 16; Tuscaloosa, AL; Valley View Baptist Church

Serve with a good attitude, as to the Lord and not to people. —Ephesians 6:7

No matter how much acclaim a person gets, the REAL praise will be when we stand before the Lord and He says, "Well done, good and faithful servant."—Tara Greene, 16; Fort Belvoir, VA; Guilford Baptist Church

In Nehemiah, the people worked hard and put all their effort toward rebuilding the wall in Jerusalem. If we are that diligent in building a relationship with God, it could be like the wall, strong and firm with a sturdy foundation and base.—Daniel Baehr, 17; Manassas, VA; Emmanuel Baptist Church

Let us run with endurance the race that lies before us, keeping our eyes on Jesus, the source and perfecter of our faith. For the joy that lay before him, he endured a cross, despising the shame, and sat down at the right hand of the throne of God.—Hebrews 12:1–2

In our relationship with Jesus, it's important to remember to keep our eyes on Him so we won't drift off and lose our way.—Emily Pitts, 16; Clearwater, FL; Calvary Baptist Church

Because of my confidence in the Word of God, I know I can, through prayer, lay all my worries and all the weight of my sin on the Lord. This allows me to start anew and again resolve to finish the race.—Mallory McClearn, 16; Leesburg, GA; Sherwood Baptist Church

The LORD is my strength and my song; he has become my salvation. This is my God, and I will praise him, my father's God, and I will exalt him.—Exodus 15:2

In tough situations when we feel as if our strength is not enough and we feel overwhelmed and overstressed, we can always find renewed strength in God.—Jacob LaValley, 16; Pageland, SC; Mount Moriah Baptist Church

Nothing can top what God has for us. God can never fail us like people can. Even our most loyal friends will let us down, but God will not!—Reagan Mi'Cole Brashears, 17; New Orleans, LA; Franklin Avenue Baptist Church

No temptation has come upon you except what is common to humanity. . . . He will also provide a way out so that you are able to bear it.—1 Corinthians 10:13

Temptation will keep you spiritually still. Every day you wake up, you wish you could shake this thing, but temptation is a stronghold, and it grows stronger every day when we do not deal with it. Don't let temptation take control of your life.—Christian Smith, 17; New Orleans, LA; Franklin Avenue Baptist Church

When you need help facing temptation, call on God. He will be happy to help.—David Atkinson, 14; Pageland, SC; Mount Moriah Baptist Church

Remember that God is the One who promises to make a way of escape for us. . . . God can do anything, so don't yield to temptation. God gives you a way to escape all temptation!

—Hunter Tremblay, 14; Pageland, SC; South Pointe Fellowship

God desires nothing more than to have a personal relationship with you. If you seek Him continuously, He will also seek you.

—Sarah Ashley Bryant, 15; Springdale, AR; Cross Church

For God has not given us a spirit of fear, but one of power, love, and sound judgment.—2 Timothy 1:7

Whether it's the big game, final exam, or even having the courage to preach the gospel, God has given us everything but a reason to fear anything we face.—Patrick Stanford, 18; Albany, GA; Sherwood Baptist Church

Guard your heart above all else, for it is the source of life.

—Proverbs 4:23

Guarding our hearts doesn't mean being cold and uncaring toward people. Jesus loves and cares for people. We should follow His example.—Tyra Ruisinger, 17; Raymore, MO; Summit Woods Baptist Church

Prayer is a powerful thing. If you are having a bad or a good day, if you are sick or healthy, if you are wealthy or poor, prayer is one of the most important parts of your relationship with God.

—Brandon Bohn, 16; Springdale, AR; Cross Church

A patient person shows great understanding, but a quick-tempered one promotes foolishness.

—Proverbs 14:29

If we learn to let go and let God handle our situations, we will experience a godly healing that pushes away anger.—T'Yanna Janai Jackson, 15; Slidell, LA; Franklin Avenue Baptist Church

God promises to take care of our needs. . . . He promised to feed, clothe, and shelter us, but He also promised to be our helper.

—Gabriel Plyler, 14; Pageland, SC; Greater Vision Baptist Church

Don't let anyone despise your youth, but set an example for the believers in speech, in conduct, in love, in faith, and in purity.—1 Timothy 4:12

To live a life being an example in purity is to guard your heart until marriage.—Nellie Otoupalik, 17; Spokane, WA; Airway Heights Baptist Church

Being young is not a limiting factor for growth in your Christian walk and involvement in sharing God's love.—Austin Southern, 17; Thailand and Mississippi; Chiang Mai Fellowship

_____

_____

_____

_____

_____

_____

_____

_____

_____

_____

_____

_____

_____

_____

_____

_____

_____

_____

_____

_____

_____

_____

Don't let your youth get in your way of serving. Remember Jeremiah who, even though he was young, served God with all he had to offer. You are never too young to serve God.—Deanna N. Davis, 3; Fairchild Air Force Base, WA; Airway Heights Baptist Church

At first, I was nervous about being a role model. But God showed me that I would be good at it as long as I was following Him.

—Sarah King, 18; Manassas; VA; Emmanuel Baptist Church

Love is patient, love is kind. Love does not envy, is not boastful, is not arrogant, is not rude, is not self-seeking, is not irritable, and does not keep a record of wrongs. Love finds no joy in unrighteousness but rejoices in the truth.—1 Corinthians 13:4–6

Wait on His perfect and pleasing plan for your life and choose to love no matter what hardships come. Choose to love no matter how you feel.—Kord Offenbacker, 16; Springdale, AR; Cross Church

Whatever you do, do it from the heart, as something
done for the Lord and not for people.—Colossians 3:23

No matter what we do, we are supposed to work at it with all our hearts, just like God was watching. Because deep down, we know He is.—Gabrielle LaCognata, 19; Belleview, FL: Church @ The Springs

_____

_____

_____

_____

_____

_____

_____

_____

_____

_____

_____

_____

_____

_____

_____

_____

_____

_____

_____

_____

_____

_____

_____

_____

The only thing that can ultimately make you happy is to follow God's will and to glorify Him with your life.—Micah Cooksey, 19; McMinnville, OR; Valley Baptist Church

Your hard work and good attitude are reflections of Christ. Do it all to glorify God! Let Him be the victor in your life all the time.

—Andrew Clem, 13; Albany, GA; Sherwood Baptist

We have to be careful about the things we do or the things we like to do. We have to make sure that we only serve God and that we are not making accidental idols.—Michaela Reed, 15; Albany, GA; Institutional First Baptist Church

Anxiety in a person's heart weighs it down, but a good word cheers it up.—Proverbs 12:25

When you focus your attention on God and trust that His Word is true, you can find peace in place of anxiety.—David Martin, 15; Lageland, SC; Mount Moriah Baptist Church

If you are discouraged, I pray this quote by Henry Ford will encourage you: "When everything seems to be going against you, remember that the airplane takes off against the wind, not with it." Even better, we have a pilot that navigates for us, so stay close to Him and soar in His strength.—Collin Michael Seelen, 18; Itami, Hyogo, Japan; Emmanuel Baptist Church

_____

_____

_____

_____

_____

_____

_____

_____

_____

_____

_____

_____

_____

_____

_____

_____

_____

_____

_____

_____

_____

_____

_____

_____

_____

_____

Fear is a very intense word that can describe a lot of situations in our lives. . . . Block out your fears today and pursue what God wants. You'll find, as I have found, that life gets a lot more enjoyable when you do.—David Josiah Woody, 16; Waynesboro, PA; Greencastle Baptist Church

Do not be conformed to this age, but be transformed by the renewing of your mind, so that you may discern what is the good, pleasing, and perfect will of God.

—Romans 12:2

Get all your knowledge from God. Don't let your soul be transformed by anyone but Jesus. —Brontë Stallings, 15; Mt. Pleasant, SC; Citadel Square Baptist Church

We do not have to mask who we are for people to like us. Don't mask who God made you. Shine and love the Lord for everything that makes you you.—Holly Kurtz, 16, Holden, MA; Bethlehem Bible Church

God's Word is a powerful weapon against the devil and his temptations. Memorizing it and quoting it during temptation is so much easier than trying to [face temptation] in our own strength.—Matthew Cooksey, 13; McMinnville, OR; Valley Baptist Church

If we are [servants] of God, then shouldn't our actions make an impact on the people around us? So be different!—Annalise Clem, 17

Albany, GA; Sherwood Baptist Church

he team member who emulates Christ will set precedence for
layers that could result in them coming to know Christ as their
ord and Savior.—Micki Werner, 16; Gatlinburg, TN; First Baptist Church

"I know the plans I have for you"—this is the LORD's declaration—"plans for your well-being, not for disaster to give you a future and a hope."—Jeremiah 29:11

We should always remember we were born to be witnesses to our generation, so we should live for Christ and serve Him forever.

–Lilian Gatheca, 15; Nanyuki, Kenya; Sherwood Baptist Church

We have a hope for all eternity.—Anna Sapone, 15; Medical Lake, WA; Airway Heights Baptist Church

_____

_____

_____

_____

_____

_____

_____

_____

_____

_____

_____

_____

_____

_____

_____

_____

_____

_____

_____

_____

_____

_____

_____

Blessed is the one who endures trials, because when he has stood the test he will receive the crown of life that God has promised to those who love him.—James 1:12

Remember that God is always there for us and that He has already won the war. As long as we keep His Word in our life, temptation will never triumph.—Jesse Nieman, 18; Ocala, FL; Church @ the Springs

If there is anything that causes you to lust, destroy it! . . . God is available in prayer and through His Word to help when the temptation to lust haunts us.—Zach Watkins, 16; Henderson, NV; Highland Hills Baptist Church

It is important that teens show God's grace to our peers as we live in front of them the way God tells us to in the Bible.

—Drew G. Jenkins, 13; Pageland, SC; Grace Baptist Church

We are called to be an example of Christ to others and share our faith with them. . . . God will surely direct the rest of your life for His glory!—Amy Meeks, 16; Tulsa, OK; Evergreen Baptist Church

Dear friends, let us love one another, because love is from God, and everyone who loves has been born of God and knows God.—1 John 4:7

Please realize God's incredible love for you. When everyone else's love fails, the love of God prevails! Love yourself and honor yourself. God made you perfectly. Spread your love.—Luke Humanik, 15; Jefferson, SC; Mt. Olive Baptist

Ask God to help you to pick your friends and to know how much time you are to give to them.—Taylor Dillon, 17; Stafford, VA; Grace Life Community Church

_____

_____

_____

_____

_____

_____

_____

_____

_____

_____

_____

_____

_____

_____

_____

_____

_____

_____

_____

_____

_____

_____

_____

This is my prayer. That when everything seems to be going wrong that I will look forward and believe that God is in control and rest in that. I hope you will make that your prayer also.—Christa Morgan, 17; Alasbaster, AL; Westwood Baptist Church

We must purposely and faithfully commit ourselves to spiritual training and prayer, constantly growing in our faith.—Connor Howington, 17; West Monroe, LA; First Baptist West Monroe

The one who guards his mouth and tongue keeps himself out of trouble.—Proverbs 21:23

Think twice before you speak and always respond in a way that glorifies the Lord.—Jonathan Dismukes, 17; Mobile, AL; Redeemer Fellowship Church

Rejoice always, pray constantly, give thanks in everything; for this is God's will for you in Christ Jesus.

—1 Thessalonians 5:16–18

God also called us to praise Him for saving us. He made the choice to save us, and we should make the choice to glorify Him for it.

—Brenna R. Strain, 15; Spokane, WA; Airway Heights Baptist Church

Our life and our praise should give glory to God for rescuing us from darkness and testimony to those in the dark world. As believers we are to shine our light!—Joel Perstrope, 15; St. Peters, MO; First Baptist Church of St. Charles

"For if you forgive others their offenses, your heavenly Father will forgive you as well. But if you don't forgive others, your Father will not forgive your offenses."
—Matthew 6:14–15

_____

_____

_____

_____

_____

_____

_____

_____

_____

_____

_____

_____

_____

_____

_____

_____

_____

_____

_____

_____

_____

_____

_____

_____

_____

Both bullies and victims need help from the one and only One who can help, God.—Terrell Strain, 13; Spokane, WA; Airway Heights Baptist Church

"Do not fear, for I am with you; do not be afraid, for I am your God. I will strengthen you; I will help you; I will hold on to you with my righteous right hand."

—Isaiah 41:10

The real world can be scary sometimes, but I have to put my faith in God and know that everything is going to be all right.—Madison Thomas, 15; Sevierville, TN; First Baptist Church

Don't you know that the runners in a stadium all race, but only one receives the prize? Run in such a way to win the prize.—1 Corinthians 9:24

If we run our race well, doing our best, when we reach the finish line there's a prize waiting for us. His name is Jesus, and He has a special crown waiting for us.—Hannah Arrington, 15; Borger, TX; First Baptist Church

We can worship God through whatever we do if we have the right attitude and are trying to do it for God's glory.—Austin Canfield, 18; Tulsa, OK; Evergreen Baptist Church

Flee from youthful passions, and pursue righteousness, faith, love, and peace, along with those who call on the Lord from a pure heart.—2 Timothy 2:22

I challenge you to rebel against rebellion and encourage your fellow believers to do the same!—Hannah Thompson, 15; Leesburg, GA; Sherwood Baptist Church

_____

_____

_____

_____

_____

_____

_____

_____

_____

_____

_____

_____

_____

_____

_____

_____

_____

_____

_____

_____

_____

_____

_____

_____

Teach us to number our days carefully so that we may develop wisdom in our hearts.—Psalm 90:12

We are here to honor and glorify God and to spread the gospel.

—Clay Norman, 18; Albany, GA; Sherwood Baptist Church

Instead of giving up, continue to persevere, and trust God that the dark will end.—Hannah Abernathie, 15; Tulsa, OK; Evergreen Baptist Church

If we would only invest more into God's stock market, we would profit from a much closer walk with Him, and our lives would be so much fuller.—Hannah Cooksey, 16; McMinnville, OR; Valley Baptist Church

*Teenagers look for acceptance in others. . . . We are to find our
acceptance in Him.*—Hailey Culberson, 17; Tulsa, OK; Evergreen Baptist Church

God is our refuge and strength, a helper who is always found in times of trouble. Therefore we will not be afraid, though the earth trembles and the mountains topple into the depths of the seas.—Psalm 46:1–2

There is no place or person on the earth that will provide a safe refuge for us and no other that can give us strength in times of trouble but God!—Hank F. Griffin, 14; Pageland, SC; White Plains Baptist Church

When you are facing the feeling of defeat, remember that there is strength and protection in the Lord.—Kyle Rape, 15; Wingate, NC; Mountain Springs Baptist Church

Strength may be that one thing we all need or desire, but not all of us have it. . . . We can't do it on our own. We can't be God, but we can let Him be our strength.—Josh Daniel, 14, Troy, OH; Two Rivers
ommunity Church

Don't be a spiritual chicken, which can barely get off the ground. Be an eagle. Soar! Soar for Christ!—Chandler Smith, 16; Springdale, AR; Cross Church

The Lord can do great things through us if we are willing to go and do what we can. He gives strength and grace to do things that our bodies couldn't do without Him. We need to trust God with our plans, and He will bring about His will in our lives.—Eli Jones, 15; Tulsa, OK; Evergreen Baptist Church

You are not to make gashes on your bodies for the dead or put tattoo marks on yourselves; I am the Lord.—Leviticus 19:28

**It hurts God when you hurt yourself.**—David Joseph Dalesandro, 14; York, SC; Hillcrest Baptist Church

Do everything without grumbling and arguing, so that you may be blameless and pure, children of God who are faultless in a crooked and perverted generation, among whom you shine like stars in the world.

—Philippians 2:14–15

God doesn't ask us to do everything without grumbling or arguing just for the fun of it. It's so that we may be blameless and pure, children of God, and so that we may "shine like stars in the world."—Isabella Bako, 14; Anchorage, AK; First Baptist Church

You reveal the path of life to me; in your presence is abundant joy; at your right hand are eternal pleasures.—Psalm 16:11

God has a plan so abundantly overwhelming for you that no one can ever imagine where it may lead. It's exciting, it's mysterious, it's captivating, and it's one of a kind.—Reagan Bell, 17; Tuscaloosa, AL; Valley View Baptist Church

After reading the Bible it's good to keep your notes to help you remember what you learned. . . . Keep your faith, pray, read the Bible daily.—Beraiah Benavides, 14; Sevierville, TN; Pathways Baptist Church

Teens tend to worry about what they are to do, but we need not worry. God will teach us and guide us.—Caleb Payne, 18; White House, TN; Long Hollow Baptist Church

[Cast] all your cares on him, because he cares about you.
—1 Peter 5:7

God wouldn't put you through something if He knew you couldn't do it.—Makenzie Thomas, 16; Sevierville, TN; First Baptist Church

Fundamentally, sin takes us further from God, causing our spiritual lives to suffer. Jesus offers us help, eternal life, meaning, and purpose.—Luke Merrick, 15; Springdale, AR; Immanuel Baptist Church

Jesus wants us, even teenagers, to be committed to prayer, trusting Him in the simple things so that we learn how to trust Him with the big things life throws at us.—Hanna Wilbourn, 14; Seymour, TN; First Baptist Church

Express excellence in whatever you choose to do with your life. He [God] is the Redeemer and Savior, and He will always be there loving us, freeing us, and restoring us.—Ife Akinboyo, 15; Seymour, TN; Sevier Heights Baptist Church

You must not spread a false report. Do not join the wicked to be a malicious witness.—Exodus 23:1

The truth sets us free and our truthful responses in difficult situations could be what causes others to want to know about Jesus.—Austin Hargett, 15; Marshville, NC; Bethel Baptist Church

Better an open reprimand than concealed love. The wounds of a friend are trustworthy, but the kisses of an enemy are excessive.—Proverbs 27:5–6

A passive friend is not a good friend. . . . The only reason you should tell on a friend is out of love, to help them because you are genuinely worried about them. They may be mad at you, but later on they will appreciate what you did for them.—Blair Bodnarchuk, 17; Raleigh, NC; Providence Baptist Church

But grow in the grace and knowledge of our Lord and Savior Jesus Christ. To him be the glory both now and to the day of eternity.—2 Peter 3:18

Growth takes work and time. We must put forth the effort to study God's Word in order to understand His grace and His will for our life. Then, we must consistently apply the truths that we learn to the glory of God.—Luke Perstrope, 17; St. Peters, MO; First Baptist Church of St. Charles

We have to work together because we need each other. When you begin to compare yourself to your "someone," keep in mind that she may be an arm and you may be a leg. Both are equally important but serve two completely different purposes in relation to the body.—Kelsey Roberts, 18; Albany, GA; Sherwood Baptist Church

Then I heard the voice of the Lord asking: Who should I send? Who will go for us? I said: Here I am. Send me.
—Isaiah 6:8

God uses those passions and characteristics [that are in us] for His glory. . . . God desires nothing more than to have our whole hearts. He wants to be able to use us in ways that we cannot imagine.—Taylor Glow, 17; Albany, GA; Sherwood Baptist Church

The one who walks with the wise will become wise, but a companion of fools will suffer harm.—Proverbs 13:20

Choose your friends wisely. It will affect your life greatly.—Hannah
Savage, 16; Dodge City, KS; First Southern Baptist Church

"When you pray, don't babble like the Gentiles, since they imagine they'll be heard for their many words."

—Matthew 6:7

Our goal should be to bring glory to God. May He give us the strength to create good habits, and may those habits never die.

—Joshua Johansen, 18; Shrewsbury, MA; Bethlehem Bible Church

Keep reaching out and wanting to be like God. It may seem difficult, but nothing is impossible with God.—Hannah Zimmerman, 16, Greencastle, PA; Greencastle Baptist Church

If someone close to you does something upsetting or snaps at you, instead of snapping back, ask how their day went. Maybe then you could understand what they're dealing with and respond the way Christ wants with love and forgiveness.—Jason McKee, 15; Anchorage, AK; First Baptist Church of Anchorage

Whether it's reading your Bible and thinking or taking time to pray and listen for God to respond, the important thing is to take that time to quiet your mind, to be still, and to know that He is God.

—Kaylin Calvert, 18; Medical Lake, WA; Airway Heights Baptist Church

We are the light of the world. As Christians, we must be a light in this dark place.—Sarah LaCognata, 14; Belleview, FL; Church @ The Springs

We can glorify God in word and deed, and people will take notice.
And that is one way God accomplishes His purpose through us!

—Kristin Goehl, 18; Princeton, MA; Bethlehem Bible Church

Forgiveness is a blessing from God. . . . Be forgiving, as God has forgiven us.—Rhett Chapman, 15; Pageland, SC; South Pointe

Are you willing to let God show you who He wants you to be for Him and to fulfill the plan He has for your life?—Rebekah Byrd, 16; Tulsa, OK; Evergreen Baptist Church

have treasured your word in my heart so that I may
not sin against you.—Psalm 119:11

We need to have the same excitement every time we read the Bible as the first time we read it and it meant something special to us. . . . We need to ask God today, without wasting a minute, to give us a hunger and thirst for His Word.—William David Orr, 17; Albany, GA; Sherwood Baptist Church

Bible study is one of the most important parts to maintaining a relationship with God. Studying God's Word every day will help us grow and mature in our walk with Christ.—Zach M. Byrd, 15; Jefferson, C; Bethlehem Baptist Church

We can't please everyone, but we can place our worries on the Lord, and He will reward us for our efforts.—Emily Matlock, 15; Springdale, AR; Cross Church

If you are wholly committed to the Lord, you will realize that complete joy is found in obedience to Him.—Danielle Quesinberry, 15; Knoxville, TN; Valley Grove Baptist Church

"Woe to the world because of offenses. For offenses will inevitably come, but woe to that person by whom the offense comes."—Matthew 18:7

don't want to be a stumbling block to anyone. We need each
other, so always remember to keep your brothers in Christ
accountable. They will be thankful for your concern and care for
them in the future.—Christopher Coleman Bailey, 17; Albany, GA; Greater
Second Mt. Olive Baptist Church

Without the spilling of Christ's blood on our behalf, we could never live in the presence of our God.—Emily Sherrod, 17; Mobile, AL; Christ Fellowship Baptist Church

By taking refuge in the Lord, we have nothing to fear!—Erin France, 4; Anchorage, AK; First Baptist Church

Don't be afraid to express your love for Jesus. People may look at you funny, but God loves it.—Breanna Smith, 17; Sharon, SC; Hillcrest Baptist Church

God wants to use you right where you are, but you must know Him and His Word to be able to hear what He is calling you to do for Him.—Reed Reynolds, 15; Albany, GA: Sherwood Baptist Church

God has not left our side, and He sees the blue skies that are waiting for us. He is walking with us through the storms and is there to be the shield of protection we need.—Haley Smith, 16; Tarpon Springs, FL; Calvary Baptist Church

There are going to be people in life who don't like you, but the Bible says many times that we should love our enemies and treat them well. Do not become like them. Instead, be the better person.—Callie Spencer, 14; Broken Arrow, OK; Evergreen Baptist Church

For you were once darkness, but now you are light in the Lord. Live as children of light.—Ephesians 5:8

We have to surrender completely to the will of God! That means everything about you! It's time for the children of God to be children of God!—Hannah McGee, 15; Springdale, AR; Cross Church

Don't be afraid or back away when someone disagrees with you on an issue, when you know it's wrong in God's eyes. That is when you need to take a stand for God.—Brianna Carter, 19; Sharon, SC; Hillcrest Baptist Church

For this reason also, since the day we heard this, we haven't stopped praying for you. We are asking that you may be filled with the knowledge of his will in all wisdom and spiritual understanding.—Colossians 1:9

Encouragement is one of the best things you can give someone. . . .
Prayer changes things, and so can you through prayer.—Imani
McBean, 14; Leesburg, GA; Mt. Zion Baptist Church

_____

_____

_____

_____

_____

_____

_____

_____

_____

_____

_____

_____

_____

_____

_____

_____

_____

_____

_____

_____

_____

More than that, I also consider everything to be a loss in view of the surpassing value of knowing Christ Jesus my Lord.—Philippians 3:8

Popularity and being accepted by others holds absolutely no eternal value, but Jesus does.—Alaina Clem, 14; Albany, GA; Sherwood Baptist Church

Whatever is true, whatever is honorable, whatever is just, whatever is pure, whatever is lovely, whatever is commendable—if there is any moral excellence and if there is anything praiseworthy—dwell on these things.

—Philippians 4:8

Those things we focus on and find entertainment in influence our heart greatly. And, what is in our hearts will reflect our actions.

—Jesse D. Sando, 13; Pleasant Hill, OH; First Baptist Church

"Love one another. Just as I have loved you, you are also to love one another. By this everyone will know that you are my disciples, if you love one another."

—John 13:34–35

Relationships are tough. . . . Scripture calls us to love our enemies and be kind to them.—Laura Roggenbaum, 17; Palm Harbor, FL; Calvary Baptist Church

Trials are presented in our lives to help us grow. Please, when you are going through hard times in your life, don't turn to anger. Turn to praise, knowing that the Lord does all things for His will, and that these trials are only to deepen your faith in Him.—Jessie Cardin, 6; Sutton, MA; Bethlehem Bible Church

This is how we know that we remain in him and he in us: He has given us of his Spirit.—1 John 4:13

God will never forsake His children and will never leave any of us in any hard situation.—Billy Ramsey, 17; Sharon, SC; Faith Baptist Church

"I have told you these things so that in me you may have peace. You will have suffering in this world. Be courageous! I have conquered the world."—John 16:33

_____

_____

_____

_____

_____

_____

_____

_____

_____

_____

_____

_____

_____

_____

_____

_____

_____

_____

_____

_____

_____

_____

_____

_____

We can't let the mistakes we make define the rest of our life.
Walking around with guilt is the last thing Jesus wants us to do.

—Victoria Davidson, 17; Newton, GA; Sherwood Baptist Church

"Go, therefore, and make disciples of all nations, baptizing them in the name of the Father and of the Son and of the Holy Spirit, teaching them to observe everything I have commanded you."—Matthew 28:19–20

It can be really hard to tell your friends and family about Christ, but I think that it should be our biggest desire for them to come to Christ because they are the ones we love most.—Micah Perstrope, 13; St. Peters, MO; First Baptist Church, St. Charles

"Stop judging according to outward appearances; rather judge according to righteous judgment."

—John 7:24

You should always get to know someone before making any assumptions about them. God looks on the heart, and we need to as well.—Faith Kurtz, 13, Holden, MA; Bethlehem Bible Church

Treasure the time with [family] now, and God will help you to share
with them.—Clara Davis, 14; Little Rock, AR; The Church at Rock Creek

Clearly, God looks at how we grow, and I think we need to take how we grow seriously and continue to strive to get to know more about our Creator!—Sara E. DuBois, 16; St. Peters, MO; First Baptist Church of St. Charles

But with you there is forgiveness, so that you may be revered.—Psalm 130:4

God does not want us to live our lives hanging on to bitterness and hate. Forgiveness is a wonderful thing, and we should not take it for granted.—Tanner Peyton, 13; Pageland, SC; Charlotte Southern Baptist

I will praise you because I have been remarkably and wondrously made. Your works are wondrous, and I know this very well.—Psalm 139:14

God loves you no matter what, and He is on your side. . . .

God is amazing and loves us more than we can even imagine.

—Allison Fisher, 14, Raleigh, NC; Providence Baptist Church

Do not love the world or the things in the world. If anyone loves the world, love of the Father is not in him.

—1 John 2:15

Keep your guard up and ask God to help you make the right choices.

—Dianah Edwards, 16; West Monroe, LA; First West Monroe Baptist Church

Christ followers will face persecution. . . . Persecution is only temporary. Whatever it may be, don't let it consume your life and steal your joy.—Carson Gregors, 17: Albany, GA; Sherwood Baptist Church

"If you have faith and do not doubt, you will not only do what was done to the fig tree, but even if you tell this mountain, 'Be lifted up and thrown into the sea,' it will be done."—Matthew 21:21

Doubt chains Christians, ruining our power to witness. . . . Always bring it to God and ask His peace and remember who you serve. . . . The doubt will pass away as your faith grows to cast it out.

—Cody Brandon, 17; Old Hickory, TN; The Fellowship of Two Rivers

If you are upset about something, just pray and ask God for comfort, and you will get that comfort. . . . So the next time you are down or need help, just remember that God is always there for you.—Michael Lowe, 15; Pageland, SC; Wolf Pond Baptist Church

One with many friends may be harmed, but there is a friend who stays closer than a brother.—Proverbs 18:24

Continuously pray to God that all of your relationships will remain strong. Most of all, pray that you will remain a good friend to your friends.—Angela Stanley, 17; Woodbridge, VA; Dale City Baptist Church

Now faith is the reality of what is hoped for, the proof of what is not seen.—Hebrews 11:1

With the knowledge that our path leads to heaven, we can relax and do what God has put us here to do—spread His Word, the gospel message!—Dylan Knoles, 13; Jefferson, SC; South Point Fellowship

Sing to the LORD, for he has done glorious things. Let this be known throughout the earth.—Isaiah 12:5

Music can be a tool to spread the gospel to all nations.

—Aaron Thompson, 13; Tiger, GA; Clayton Baptist Church

But each person is tempted when he is drawn away and enticed by his own evil desires. Then after desire has conceived, it gives birth to sin, and when sin is fully grown, it gives birth to death.—James 1:14–15

Seek the Lord by knowing God and His Word, by praying, by being open with our parents, and by surrounding ourselves with Christian friends for accountability.—Paul Richardson, 17; Huntsville, AL; Whitesburg Baptist Church

God will give you His strength to overcome the temptations that Satan throws at you. God is greater, and He wants to aid us in all areas of temptation. Call on Him, day or night.—Joshua Cooksey, 15; McMinnville, OR; Valley Baptist Church

"God loved the world in this way: He gave his one and only Son, so that everyone who believes in him will not perish but have eternal life"—John 3:16

God is there for you. He wants you to have a relationship with Christ and to know how to pray in the good times and bad.

—Paul Craig Gale, 14; New Orleans, LA; Franklin Avenue Baptist Church

Everyone with a proud heart is detestable to the LORD;
be assured, he will not go unpunished.—Proverbs 16:5

Christians are to always be humble, and when we do fall short and become proud then we have to ask God for His help.—Raj Patel, 15; Jefferson, SC; South Pointe Fellowship

n God, whose word I praise, in the Lᴏʀᴅ, whose word praise, in God I trust; I will not be afraid. What can mere humans do to me?—Psalm 56:10–11

Are you willing to be fearless for the cause of Christ?—Jackson Reese, 18; Pageland, SC; South Pointe Fellowship

Listen to counsel and receive instruction so that you may be wise later in life.—Proverbs 19:20

Jesus is the #1 mentor for life, so look to Him before you look to anyone else.—Trey Suey, 16; Mt. Juliet, TN; The Fellowship at Two Rivers

When you are in need of something, ask God and then seek it out in your life.—Kyle Sutton, 16, Pageland SC; First Baptist Church

"But I say to you who listen: Love your enemies, do what is good to those who hate you, bless those who curse you, pray for those who mistreat you."—Luke 6:27–28

Find one person, and befriend them. God has called us to love everyone, no matter how hard it may be. The blessing will be theirs and yours, and you might make a friend for all eternity!

—Layne Coleman, 14; Little Rock, AR; The Church at Rock Creek

Once you begin to delight in the Lord, you begin to think more like God, and then your desires become what God wants for you. Those are the desires that God will grant you.—Dustin Brecht, 17; Lancaster, SC; Spring Hill Baptist Church

God's brilliance and creativity shine forth in the entire world around us.—Luke Abendroth, 16; Lancaster, MA; Bethlehem Bible Church

The Bible is more than a book of rules. The Bible has rules in it that are extremely important, but it also tells a story.—Chris Nation, 15; Gallatin, TN; The Fellowship at Two Rivers

For am I now trying to persuade people, or God? Or am I striving to please people? If I were still trying to please people, I would not be a servant of Christ.

—Galatians 1:10

"Love your neighbor as yourself. There is no other command greater than these."—Mark 12:31

God wants us to love everyone no matter how badly they treat you or how hard it can be. Remember that God has told us to love our enemies.—Michaela Reed, 15; Albany, GA; Institutional First Baptist Church

There is one who speaks rashly, like a piercing sword; but the tongue of the wise brings healing.—Proverbs 12:18

Words are powerful, and they have the ability to either lift up or destroy. . . . Hold your tongue and think before you speak. People are watching you. Make everything you say count.—Hannah McGee, 5; Springdale, AR; Cross Church

"Haven't I commanded you: be strong and courageous? Do not be afraid or discouraged, for the LORD your God is with you wherever you go."—Joshua 1:9

No matter what people say, you are always good enough, and our awesome God has an amazing plan for you.—Trey Suey, 16; Mt. Juliet, TN; The Fellowship at Two Rivers

Put your faith in God, and He will not only give you endurance but also keep you from falling.—Kelsey Roberts, 18; Albany, GA; Sherwood Baptist Church

"Go home to your own people, and report to them how much the Lord has done for you and how he has had mercy on you."—Mark 5:19

You are in your own mission field right now, surrounded by people who need to feel God's love. Go and proclaim what Jesus has done for you. . . . Just because you aren't in a different part of the world doesn't mean you can't help others into the kingdom of God.—Zach Watkins, 16; Henderson, NV; Highland Hills Baptist Church